RESERVATION

VOLUME 2, ISSUE 1 OF BRAIN BOOSTER ARTICLES

SAIMA HASAN

Contents

Preface

"Start writing, no matter what. The water does not flow until the faucet is turned on".

-Louis L'Amour

Hundreds of students and professors are contributing their work to Brain Booster Articles, we are here to provide ample information about Law and Contemporary issues. Our aim is to provide a platform for today's generation to express their views and ideas on law and contemporary law.

Publication

This research paper is publication in volume 2, issue 1 of Brain Booster Articles

CHAPTER ONE

ABSTRACT

The following research paper consist of the essence of reservation in India and the source from which it draw it`s existence. Reservation was give to impoverished people with the motive to match their capabilities with those of others. Well will here discuss the detail of reservation and will analyze it`s impact in today`s society.

CHAPTER TWO

INTRODUCTION

Caste reservation is one the most controversial issues that has been going on in the country since years should government give reservations on the basis of caste? or should it not?. The question is quite simple, but when you try answering it, a lot complexities get involved.

The topic of caste based reservation would remain incomplete if we do not mention caste based reservation, here I want to ask you question how much discrimination is done on the basis of caste relevant today? Is untouchability practiced even today? For those who live in big cities, they might presume that this is only limited to bookish information and it is not practiced in today`s times. You would be surprised to know that in districts of Uttar Pradesh, Bihar and Madhya Pradesh, the ratio is more than 50%. In 2016, SARI Social Attitude Research India conducted a phone survey in Delhi Mumbai, Rajasthan to ask how many of them saw discrimination taking place in their homes or how they practiced discrimination themselves, 39% of the Non-Dalit Hindu women admitted that someone in their household practiced untouchability , 21% of the Non-Dalit Hindu women that they themselves practiced untouchability. Around 60% Non-Dalits in Rajasthan believe that inter caste marriages should be abolished. In the same survey, 43% of respondents from Delhi said that they opposed reservation and argued that seats should be allotted on the basis of merit and not on the basis of caste.

So the argument of those who support based reservation is that caste based discrimination exists even today so there should be caste based reservation and those who are against it argue that seats should be allotted on the basis of merit and that the caste based reservation undoes the equality in society.

CHAPTER THREE

ORIGIN OD CASTE SYSTEM

There are several theory behind caste the origin of the caste system. According to a theory found in Rig Veda, the first humans in our universe destroyed themselves to create our society. People of different categories that is, " Varna" came out of their different body parts. For example from the head came out Brahmans-the intelligent and knowledgeable ones and it is believed that they are responsible for our education, from their arms came out the Kshatriyas- that were powerful and strong and hence considered as warriors, from their thighs came out the Vaishyas-the traders and from their feet came out the Shudras that do menial jobs in our society. One category is missing from the entire system-that of the Dalits because they are not even in the classification this is why they are called "Avarnas" people who do not have any varna and they are given the task of cleansing.

Another theory suggest that your caste depends on the deeds of your past life, so, if you did good deeds in your past life, you would be born as a Brahman in this life and if you did not do good deeds in your past life you would be born as a Dalit in this life. According to this theory if a lower caste person to be born into an upper caste in his next life then they should work dutifully within their own caste.

With passage of time, this caste system became more rigid and caste rules can be seen anywhere. What work you do, who do you marry, what temples do you go to and whom do you eat with all this dependent on caste and people could not been shunned their caste identities which is why, several lower caste people become Buddhists in the 6th century. Gautam Buddha, who himself was Kshatriyas was also against this caste system. And this conversion in Buddhism was not seen only in the 6th century but also in 1956,B.R Ambedkar was a part of mass conversion in which around 5lakh lower caste Hindus converted to Buddhism.

CHAPTER FOUR

BRITISH INFLUENCE

After the coming of British, this entire system has changed and become even more discriminatory and rigid. The reason behind this is simple, British wanted to make the task of administrating India more simple. For British the entire system was extremely complex and so they wanted to simplify it. James Prince who was British scholar who was conducting the census of 1834 he found out that even in the Brahmans of Benaras, there were more than 107 distinct castes. For the 1872 census, Waterfield thought that it would be easier to classify Indians along the four Varna system. Everyone today knows about the four Varna system- it is that popular, but W.R Cornsih who was responsible for the census of Madras, In 1871 gave a very famous statement-"It is doubtful that there was any period during which the Hinduswere composed of the four castes only. He believed that historically, no such period existed when Hindus were divide only into four categories and that even more divisions existed. So British popularized the four Varna system in which the Brahmans were classified at the top as the privileged class. Warren Hastings took initiative in 1772 to formulate the Hindu Muslim law, for this he hired 11 Brahmans Pandits, who took advantage of the situation and applied Vedic laws even more widely this is called "Brahmanism"or "Brahmanwaad" that forced upon the Hindus until then, the Vedic system of our four system was not so widely practiced and nor did every Hindu practice it was forcefully imposed. M.N Srinivas and Indian sociologist describes how the British Raj made socially mobility even more difficult, the intermingling of people from different castes become even more difficult after the advent of the British. Earlier, it was possible for people belonging to castes other than Brahmans to gain political power, but the British made this even more difficult. For example, Lord Hardinge, the viceroy of India in 1910s decided all the seats in public services would be filled up by an open competition exam, which would be conducted in English, this was a huge advantage for the Brahmans of the Madras Presidency because they were the sole ones who had the privileged access of learning this language. Due to this, Brahmans in Madras(who compromised only 3% of the population there) occupied more than 80% of the posts, so, in the princely states of Mysore, the Tamil Brahmans monopolized all the jobs.

CHAPTER FIVE

PRE-INDEPENDENCE

There were a lot of people in the late 19th and 20th century who took concrete measures against our caste system. SahujiMaharaj was the first person in India to implement reservation in Kolhapur region. JyotiraoPhule, who was born in the Shudra caste, was very inspired by the struggle of slaves in America. In 1873, he established the "SatyashodhakSamaj" for the upliftment of the lower castes. He refused the sacrosanct ness of the Vedas and refused to believe that only the Brahmans should have control over Hindu religion. The biggest contribution in the 20th century against caste system has arguably been that of B.R Ambedkar who has written popular books like "Annihilation of caste" and " The emancipation of untouchables", he was also demanding separate representation for the lower castes that he also referred to as "oppressed" or "depressed" class. Separate representation not just against the British, but also against the Brahmans, in 1930 Nagpur he organized a Depressed Classes Congress and declared that for the safety of the Depressed Classes, their need for independence from the British as well as the congress. In August 1932, British Prime Minister Ramsay MacDonald accepted the demands of Dr.Ambedkar and decided to allot sepertae electorates for the depressed classes, under which all minorities namely, Mohammadians, Parsis, Anglo-Indian and depressed classes were being granted a separate electorate. When Gandhi Ji heard that British had granted separate electorate to Dalits, he announced a fast unto death, because he believed that this policy was creating a chasm between Harijans and the rest of the Hindus. But Dr. Ambedkarremained unmoved he believed a separate representation was the was the way to upliftment of the depressed classes, but deteriorating health of Gandhi Ji closed all options but to negotiation which is called as "Poona Pact" and Gandhi Ji reassured him that instead of separate electorates, more reservations could be provided for the depressed classes in the joint electorates, so, the seats reserved for them were increased to 148 after the Poona Pact. A lot of people believe that had Dalits been granted a separate electorates, then their situation would been granted today.

CHAPTER SIX

POST INDEPENDENCE

Post Independence, the depressed classes were given reservation and political representation in both public as well as public employment, for political representation, the system of join electorates continued. This is why out the 543 Lok Sabha seats 84 seats have reserved for Schedule Castes and 47 have reserved for Scheduled Tribes. Apart from this, when the constitution was being drafted in 1950, Article 15 and 16 were in it which allow special provisions being granted to uplift the socially and educationally backward classes in terms of education and public employment. In proportion to population,15% of the seats are reserved for scheduled castes and 7.5% of seats are reserved for scheduled tribes today. Before 1993, reservation only existed for the scheduled castes and scheduled tribes but post 1993, reservation were extended for the other backward as well as after the Mandal Commission report. As per the report, 27% reservations were granted to OBCs in the government jobs and alter educational institutions as well which brought the percentage of reserved seats under the central government to total 49.5%. as for the state government, they were given the powers to extend the reservations for the rest of the communities. In 2019 these reservations went one step ahead and granted 10% reservations to economically weaker sections belonging to general category in the higher educational institutes which brought total reservations to almost 60%.

CHAPTER SEVEN

WHAT HAS BEEN THE IMPACT OF CASTE RESERVATION?

First we have to talk about the outcome in higher education. In Article 15 and 16 of the constitution has give the powers to our government to reserve seats in educational institutes and in matters of public employment. According to population share, about 22% seats have been reserved for SCs and STs, so the first question is has reservation resulted in increased representation of the SCs and STs? From 1970 to 1990, this representation has increased for both the groups and according to latest higher education survey this representation has increased further as well. But can we say with utmost guarantee that reservation is the reason behind the increase in representation? It is possible that the economic growth in India, SCs and STs have been uplifted more and this is the reason behind the increase in their representation. If we want, we can speak of it possibilities but as told by researchers, we cannot say with guarantee that reservation only is responsible for it. Despite the increase we must focus on the fact that the representation share of STs is still lower than their reservation number. One the most common criticism of reservation is of creamy layer, according to this theory,the SCs and STs that do get reservation do not belong to some poor family but are infact from rich family and because of the reservation, the people belonging to poorer section from the general category do not get seats. SC and ST do get reservation are better off in their own group but their situation is not better than general category people. The argument given against the reservation in education is that the reserved students have lesser score requirements. This might help them get a seat but after getting into the college, they would struggle and this would be wasted. In a research conducted in 215 engineering colleges, it was found that there isn`t any evidence that suggested that reserved students are not able to coup up with the syllabus.

According to government data, there has been an increase in representation of SCs and STs in government administration. But when we look at this data in detail and divide the government positions in different levels, we see that SCs and STs have representation but it is mostly in lower positions. For example their representation in near their representation quota only in group C and D category. SCs have higher representations in group D positions because many of these people Are sanitation workers, in fact, 40% sanitation workers are SCs. One more argument that is quoted against the reservation in government jobs that if people from the marginal group enter governance then the effectiveness of governance will be compromised. To study this argument two researchers have studied the data of Indian Railways from 1980 to 2000 and found out there is no such evidence, but in some cases they found out that efficiency has increased because of reserved employees.

Reservation has resulted in the increased representation of disadvantaged groups in public administration and higher educational institutes but what has been the impact in their lives? According to research, overall there has been a positive impact in their lives but there is lot of room for improvement even now. For example the post reservation in government jobs, the representation of SCs and STs in salaried jobs increased by 5%. Due to reservation on an average a student stared studying for 0.8 years and more. If we talk about reservation in political seats there we see a mixed impact, reservation in gram panchayat has resulted in decrease in poverty amongst the STs but there is no such impact in schedule caste.

If we look at all these studies then you feel like that reservation is quite a good policy in so many positive changes but we should also remember that reservation cannot change everything and we have seen certain examples that reservation wouldn`t necessarily result in changing the undercurrent of the society. Many researchers have talked about the same as well that including quotas in political representation do not guarantee benefit to marginal communities, to win a panchayat election, a leader needs support from different social groups and this is the reason that many times they would not take such decision that will only help their group.

CHAPTER EIGHT

CONCLUSION

Despite these benefits of reservation, there is a huge gap between lower caste and upper caste people today. Data from 2011 shows that a brahman adult on am average acquires 5.6 years of more education over the course of his lifetime as compared to scheduled tribe adult. All these arguments and data prove that only caste reservation is not enough to solve the problem of caste discrimination in our country.

Greater social integration means that people from different caste live together in every aspects of life, not just live in same society but also participate in similar activities and inter castemarriages also should rise, according to me schools are the best example of social integration. And if such interaction happen more in school and colleges then inter-caste marriages will automatically rise in the country consequently resulted in decrease in discrimination. Prevention of Atrocities Act 1995, tries to protect SCs and STs from discrimination, but the evidence has suggested that the provision of this act is barely been utilized, with low conviction and back log of cases. Another good example of improving the system is not only provide reservation but also free coaching classes to marginalized groups. One such scheme was launched by Ministry of Social Justice and Empowerment in 2016 where SCs and STs were offered free coaching classes for UPSC, NEET, JEE. It was reported that more than 10% percent of students who availed the benefits of this scheme cracked these exams.

www.ingramcontent.com/pod-product-compliance
Ingram Content Group UK Ltd.
Pitfield, Milton Keynes, MK11 3LW, UK
UKHW021926190726
13853UKWH00002B/872

9 798886 298772